POP'S BOOK FOR THE GENERATIONS

Pop's Book for the Generations

56 Years of Making Mistakes and the Cheat Codes You Need to Avoid Them

Christopher Robert Weir

©2025 All Rights Reserved. No portion of this book may be reproduced, stored in a retrieval system, or transmitted in any form or by any means- electronic, mechanical, photocopy, recording, scanning, or other-except for brief quotations in critical reviews or articles without the prior permission of the author.

Published by Game Changer Publishing

Paperback ISBN: 978-1-967424-25-2

Hardcover ISBN: 978-1-967424-26-9

Digital: ISBN: 978-1-967424-27-6

www.GameChangerPublishing.com

I dedicate this book to my three children, Courtney, Jessica, and Christopher Jr. As a father who is also a business owner, entrepreneur, and sometimes motivational speaker, I have been able to find or create moments of quiet contemplation at various times in my life. And invariably, when I find these moments, I ask myself the all-important question, "What do I want in life most?" The answer is, I want my three children to be proud of me.

Thank you, guys, for enriching my life every day.

A special thank you to my wife, Kim, who lifts me up every day and always manages to say the things that every man should get to hear. Together, we hope to provide a vision of what a healthy marriage can be for my three and her two adult children, Payton and Erynn.
Thank you, Kim, for helping me agonize over every word in my writing and for taking the time to write my Foreword.

READ THIS FIRST

CONNECT WITH THE AUTHOR

Scan the QR code to connect directly with the author!
Ask questions, share your thoughts about the book,
or just say hello—your feedback is always welcome.

Scan the QR Code Here:

POP'S BOOK FOR THE GENERATIONS

56 YEARS OF MAKING MISTAKES AND THE CHEAT CODES YOU NEED TO AVOID THEM

CHRIS WEIR

FOREWORD

A visionary is a person who thinks about or plans the future with imagination or wisdom, with original ideas about what the future will or could be like.

My husband is such a visionary. Chris has been able to build and run a business that is still enduring after 33 years. He created the life he envisioned, where he gets to see and work with his brothers, his mother, and his three adult children every day. He is a big believer in the saying, "If you can dream it, you can achieve it," and he is an example of that.

I married a dreamer, a romantic, and an endless optimist. That is who your dad or POP really is. He wants nothing more than to spend time with his TEAM.

I am grateful beyond measure to get to share a life with him.

– Kimberly Weir

CONTENTS

Introduction	xiii
1. Question Everything and Find a Better Way to Do Anything	1
2. What Do You Want Most?	9
3. Be Nice No Matter What	17
4. It's the Tough Things That Teach You	23
5. If You Don't Like What You're Doing, So What?	31
6. Seek Improvement Everywhere and in All Things	35
7. Stand out From the Crowd	39
8. Take People With You on Your Journey	43
9. Work-Life Balance	49
10. If You're Going to Do Anything, Do It All the Way	53
11. Give Back to Everyone You Can	59
12. Heal Yourself With Your Mind	63
Conclusion	71

INTRODUCTION
THE QUESTION IS, WHO AM I?

I'm Pop, and I raised one of your parents. There are some things I think you should know about me, but I think there are some things you ought to know that you can take with you forever. By the time you read this, I have no idea what format it will be. Bookstores are going away all the time, so maybe you'll be reading this on a computer screen or wearing a pair of glasses that show the book's pages. Maybe technology will simply read the book to you, and with artificial intelligence, you could overlay my voice as well. What a wonderful time we live in, but I think everyone should say that about their time.

Let me tell you a story from my time. If you're old enough, I think you'll like it. It's probably hard to think of your Pop as a first grader, but like everyone, I was once six years old. We were living on Long Island, New York, and had not yet moved to Texas. I can tell you that this was one of my parents' favorite stories. The only reason I know the story is because my dad loved to tell it. I have no memory of it other than their telling of it. As I entered the cafeteria for lunch, I got into the lunch line. A large man, the gym teacher, came over and tapped me on the shoulder as I was just standing in line, minding my own business. "Son," he said, "I need you to go to the back of the line. You cut the line." It was called "cutting the line" back then when you put yourself in line in front of everyone else. He told me I had cut in front of other people, to which I replied, "No, I didn't cut, and I won't go to the back of the line." The teacher was surprised that a six-year-old would challenge his authority so boldly, but he collected himself and demanded again that I head to the back of the lunch line. I replied with the same answer. "I did not cut the line, and I won't go to the back." Ultimately, he accepted my answer and did not put me at the back of the line, but he asked me to see him in the back of the lunchroom after I finished my lunch. Upon finishing my lunch, however, I simply went back to class.

I didn't follow his request because, at that moment, I didn't deem it necessary. I thought to myself, as a six-year-old, *Was this right or was this wrong?* And to me, it was wrong. So I went back to class.

That wasn't the end of it, though, because the school involved my parents. The next day, I was summoned down to the principal's office(a foreshadowing of my middle school future)and was confronted by the principal and my parents, Bill and Lucy. My parents were not happy about having to change their plans to go to the school to find out why their youngest son was "acting out." But there they sat, listening to the entire story from the principal's side. Once they had heard his recounting of what happened, my father stood up and said, "Well, it sounds like he didn't cut the line, so he wasn't going to go to the back of the line." And that was the end of the story.

My parents told that story for years and years to come. I believe it helped shape me as a person who values free thinking. My parents could have scolded me and taught me to listen to my elders and not make trouble, but instead, they supported my standing up for myself to an authority figure. And a big one at that, in the form of our male gym teacher! I imagine him to be six foot six, but he was likely five foot five and just seemed tall because I was only six.

The story shows that even at an early age, I was already thinking for myself, sticking up for myself (even to an authority figure), and thinking about what was right and what was wrong. Now, again, I can only assume I didn't cut in line, as I don't remember. It can be challenging to think about right and wrong and take the best path, the right path, and not just accept what somebody says is true.

And that's why I want to talk to you in my book. Writing this book was difficult because there are many things I want you to know, and I wondered how I could condense them all into just one book. But although I knew how difficult it would be to write this, I knew I needed to do it to create a wonderful opportunity for you to learn a bit about me, my parents, and my brothers—all amazing people you should know about.

You are why I'm writing this book. This book is for you—my children, grandchildren, and great-grandchildren. I hope to give you a head start on what I think is very important. You may agree with some of the things I tell you, or you may not, and that's okay. But I hope you don't just take it all. I hope you realize that this is information you can either keep and add to the knowledge you already have or let go. That will be the case with every book you read—ask yourself, "Does it make sense, and do you agree?"

What could turn out to be the most essential part of this book is reminding my children and grandchildren that when raising your kids, it's important not to squash their critical thinking skills. It's important to always be thinking. Give them those skills. Help them to nurture those skills. Don't make every decision for them. Thinking doesn't mean being stressed out, and it doesn't mean worrying. In this book, I hope to give my future generations a look into who I am, how I think, and what I think is important. I hope to give you guys a few good stories from my past and maybe spark one or two ideas for your journey.

When I was seven, my family moved to Texas. We lived there for five years before moving on to Scottsdale, Arizona. It was in Scottsdale where my father, who often worked out of the house, asked me to come upstairs to his office to help him with some work. I vividly remember just how much I disappointed my father at this time. I bet he didn't remember this occasion because my father had a knack for remembering only the good stuff and letting go of the bad stuff, but I never forgot his message. He was folding papers, putting them in envelopes, addressing them, and putting stamps on them. He asked me to help him.

When I was thirteen years old and in seventh grade, I was always busy doing something that I'm sure wasn't important at all. After riding the school bus home, I was ready to lie on the carpet in front of the television to watch the old Batman and Robin TV show starring Adam West that ran right after school. I remember it like it was yesterday. I would get home and plop down on the living room floor with an oversized stuffed pillow—it was a comfortable spot. Mom would come in and deliver snacks to me in front of the television. My favorite snack then was a chocolate Suzy Q (google it).

Okay, so let's get back to my story of disappointment. When helping my father, I burned through the work as quickly as possible so that I could run back downstairs to see what foul villain Batman and Robin would be facing that day. The letters were not folded evenly. The stamps were not put in the proper location and weren't straight. Some may have even been hanging off the end of the envelope. When I finished and handed the envelopes back to my father, he looked at me and asked me why I couldn't have just taken a few minutes to slow down and do it properly. And he said those famous and trite words, "Anything worth doing is worth doing well."

It's interesting because growing up, so many things happened —so many things, so many stories, so many moments in time —and there are these few snapshots in your life that you can remember like it was yesterday, this being one of them. I remember handing my father those envelopes that were so poorly put together with stamps hanging off the end, and I remember the look on his face. *A job worth doing is a job worth doing well.* I never forgot this moment, and this one has guided me in everything I have tried to do. If I was going to do something, I was going to do it as well as I could. I hope you do, too, as you grow and take on tasks or hobbies. Why do it halfway? What would Pop say? He would say to do it right, and you will be glad you did.

It was just a moment. Dad could have left me down there to watch whatever television show I was watching, but he asked me to come up and help him, and in doing so, it made a difference. It created a moment that I still remember today, forty-five years later. In learning a bit about your father, grandfather, or great-grandfather, you'll realize that there are so many things you can do in the world—anything you can conceive of, anything you can think of, anything you can put in your mind that opens you and expands your thoughts. You can make a few dollars. You can change a few lives. You can change the world around you. You can change the world. I hope these little notes I offer you will open your mind to many different things and possibilities. The things you can accomplish—alone or with a team—will be worth it. I am your Pop.

ONE
QUESTION EVERYTHING AND FIND A BETTER WAY TO DO ANYTHING

This is one of my favorite concepts. Questioning everything doesn't mean disagreeing with everything. It doesn't mean that at all. Questioning everything means just the opposite. Questioning everything doesn't mean you're trying to prove somebody else wrong. The context is critical when we question everything. You don't have to question somebody who says something you want to challenge. You might question it internally. I think the best way for me to describe it is if you're trying to prove yourself to be right, then you're questioning things for the wrong reason. When you question, you're not trying to prove anything. You're trying to *im*prove it. If you can get somewhere faster, if you can get somewhere safer, if you can accomplish something quicker, then maybe you can move on to something bigger that you might have been thinking about.

My company had finally started growing, and it was time to start hiring people. In today's work environment, you can look for job candidates in several ways. You can go online to platforms like Indeed, ZipRecruiter, or others. You can place an ad on LinkedIn, or you can post on social media sites. Back then, you could use a hiring service or run an ad in the local newspaper. I did what most people did—I ran an ad in the classified ads at the back of the newspaper. This is what the paper looked like—a sea of ads all basically saying the same thing.

Everyone did that back then, so I thought it must work. I set out to write an ad that said just about the same thing as every other ad: *"Hiring for mail shop workers, full-time work in Grapevine, Texas, call Lead Concepts at 817-421-5803."* Now, I didn't love that message, but that was the template. I sent the ad off to the Denton County newspaper at a cost of what I believe was about $200, and within a week, the ad was displayed in the back of the paper. For some reason, that ad did not draw any phone calls. We did not get a single job applicant from it, so I decided to leave it in the paper for another week. But the results were the same. I learned a valuable lesson, and it only cost me two weeks of running that ad —$400 in total. I decided I'd have to do the exact opposite of everyone else who had an ad running, so this time, I set out to craft an ad that would stand out, an ad that couldn't be ignored. There was no rule that said I had to hire one full-time person. What if I hired two or three part-time people? And, rather than asking for full-time workers, what if I offered flexible part-time hours? And instead of hiding how much I was willing to pay for those hourly wages, what if I stated in the ad exactly how much I would pay, which no one else did?

Since we were a small company, one of the things we often did was listen to the radio while we were working. We always tuned in to a sports radio show that was very popular at the time. So I ran the ad on that station, Sportsradio 1310 The Ticket, all day long while we were working. I created that ad, and I showed it to a couple of people in my office, and they said it was crazy. They told me I couldn't post that, and I asked them why. What was the worst that could happen? If it didn't work, well, the other ads didn't work either. So I did it. I published that ad. "Flexible hours, $11 an hour, we listen to sports radio while we're working."

We got so many phone calls! So many people called, and we had so many interviews. We hired more people than we set out to hire. One thing I learned is if you find quality people, you want to bring them in. And if you have quality people who want to work, you hire them.

By doing exactly the opposite of what everybody else was doing—publishing my revamped advertisement for the same price as the old one—the results were completely different. I assumed as a young man that if everyone was doing it one way, it had to be the best way. Not true. I hope that you grow up and learn these concepts, not just from me but from other books you read, other information you gather, and by paying attention to life itself right in front of you. I hope my grandchildren and great-grandchildren will look at everything and ask themselves, "Does it make sense to do it this way?" If I didn't skip in line, do I need to go to the back of the line? If everyone publishes an ad this way, does that make it the best way?

The point here is not to prove that everybody else is wrong but simply to improve your process. Does it make sense to do it this way? Is there a better way? We were hiring for one full-time, but we could be hiring for two part-time or three. This same concept just showed up again thirty years later. As my company has started hiring virtual employees (team members who don't work or live in our city), we've found it very difficult to keep these virtual team members working all day long. I looked at the situation and said to myself, *Well, the system isn't working because we're hiring remote people, and we can't tell if they're working.* It seemed like we were only getting about half a day's work from them. So I asked whether we should just hire them for half a day.

Flexible hours again. The program worked exceptionally well once we moved it to a flexible-hour situation. We tend to focus on doing things a certain way because that's what we think we're supposed to do, and there's nothing wrong with that. It's normal. But when you get a chance to take a deep breath and say, "Wait a minute, this isn't working, we need to ask why it's not working. Does it make sense to do it this way? Is there a better way to do it?" It's about asking yourself why something is done in a certain way. "Do we need a full-time person, or do we need competent help where we can find it?"

Disagreeing with your gym teacher or a doctor, though, can produce a tougher argument.

As a tennis player in college and beyond, I developed, just as my father had, a smooshed black toenail. That toenail would not grow back properly, no matter how long I waited, and at times, it would hurt. Beyond that, it wasn't pretty to look at. My mom finally told me to make an appointment with a podiatrist (foot doctor). I agreed, called the doctor, and made an appointment. He was a nice gentleman, a businessman, an entrepreneur who happened to be a doctor with a small practice. His office was in a little shopping center with an Ace Hardware store tucked between his office and a donut shop. I remember that the doctor was friendly and knowledgeable but serious. His office was mostly empty at the time, with no assistant to answer the phones, but there was a repairman who was trying to fix his computer. He took me into a small exam room, had me sit on a table covered by a thin sheet of white paper, and asked me to remove my shoe and sock. After looking at my disfigured black toe, he stated that the nail would likely not grow back correctly and would continue to cause pain. "The proper course of action," said the serious doctor, "is to kill the nerves around the toenail and remove that toenail forever."

I thought it was drastic. This guy takes one look at my disgusting black toenail and wants to disfigure me forever. In my mind, he was more worried about fixing his printer and what that would cost. I knew it was just a toenail, but I disagreed with his assessment. If I didn't do it, and it kept bothering me, I could do it later. But he was a specialist. Was I going to embarrass him by telling him I didn't agree or just let him kill part of me? He left the exam room, and it took him a bit longer to come back in than I thought it would, but that was because the computer repairman was trying to help him fix whatever was wrong with his computer.

When he found his way back to me, he was prepared to remove my toenail and, in my mind, disfigure what, quite frankly, was already a not-very-attractive foot. I looked at him and told him I disagreed with his assessment and would rather he not remove my toenail forever. If my foot continued to hurt, I could always come back in three months, six months, or a year to have it removed. And he agreed. I paid him about $75 for an office visit, and then I was off with my disfigured toe. I relayed that story to my mother, who said, "You know, there's a product I've seen at the drugstore. It's called 'Outgrow,' and you can put these drops on the skin around your toenail. It's supposed to make the skin harder and help your toenail grow out." So I went to the store and put that on my toenail every day as the instructions indicated, and within a month or two, that toenail had grown out completely. As I write this book today, I'm fifty-six years old and still have a toenail. My feet are not beautiful, neither are my toes, but they have nails. And I think my foot is just a little bit less gross because it has a nail rather than not. And I will tell you a secret—as I write this book today, my right toenail is black. My answer has been to wear socks.

There's a winding maze of running trails behind my house, and there are bikers and runners. And the rules of the road on the trails are that everybody goes in the same direction, but the bikes move at a much faster pace than the runners or walkers. I've run on the trails many, many times and find it particularly dangerous if a biker comes up very quickly behind me and I can't hear him. But the rules of the road on the trails are that everyone goes in the same direction.

I see that as putting me in danger. It's not mortal danger, but I'd rather not get run over by a bicycle and hurt my leg or sprain a knee or tear my shoulder. At this point, I've had three surgeries on my right shoulder from my tennis history. So, I've chosen to go against the rules, but I studied it beforehand. If I'm going toward a biker, I can see and hear the biker much quicker than if I'm going with traffic. When I head against the traffic on the trails, it's safer for me and safer for the biker. The rule doesn't make sense to me. When you run on the road, you run toward traffic so you can step off the road if a car is coming. It's the same concept for me on the trails, but for some reason—and there may be a reason that I just don't know—I'm supposed to run with the traffic. Maybe if I knew why it was that way, it would help me to follow that rule. But it doesn't make sense to do something that's not safe. I want to run, enjoy my time on the trails, and not be worried about getting run over.

Some people disagree with me about going toward the traffic, but it's a better way to do it. I've looked at it, and I've studied it. I'm a free thinker, and that just makes more sense. I hope you don't see questioning everything as being negative or argumentative. Think of questioning everything simply as a way to improve yourself, your choices, your life, and the things around you. And as things show up in your life that may or may not seem to be obstacles, start by asking yourself a few questions. And yes, think about Pop because he is thinking about you right now.

TWO
WHAT DO YOU WANT MOST?

People often talk about the things they want in life. I do that quite often, especially when I was younger. I talked about all the things that I wanted to do, all the things that I wanted in life. And the thing I didn't understand as a young man is that it didn't really matter what I wanted until I asked myself what I wanted the *most*. You see, without the word *most* in there, it's too broad. There are so many things we all want, but none of them are things we need. And that's okay—I'm not saying not to want things. But it's important to stop and find a quiet place to think about that one thing you want the *most*—and the word *most* changes the meaning completely. Because when you boil it down to just one thing, if you're willing to go after that one thing, you will achieve it no matter what it is, whether it's faith or family or relationships or lots of money or being super fit. Don't let anybody tell you what you want because it's deeply personal. Only you get to decide that. But it's important to decide and then determine whether you're willing to do the things you need to do that take you down the path to achieving it or finding happiness in the pursuit of that one thing.

Remember that your life isn't only about you; it's about everybody else in your circle—your mom, your dad, your siblings, and as you get older, your spouse and your own children. Life for me has been more about lifting up others whenever I can find a way to do it. What I want *most* in life has changed a few times, and now what I want *most* is for my children, Courtney, Jessica, and Christopher (CJ), to be proud of me. I receive the most joy in life by providing for the people I love and making sure they're getting what they want. You can only hope that what you want *most* is in some way in alignment with what they want.

We called my grandmother (my father's mother) Nanny. She was a tough woman. She raised seven kids on the Lower East Side of New York City during the '40s and '50s, which were some tremendously difficult times. Unfortunately, we didn't get to spend a lot of time with Nanny, but I remember her saying, "Oh, stop your whining." Stop complaining, is what she was saying. Complaining will get you nowhere. Pay attention to what matters. Look forward to what you're trying to accomplish, and what you said was the *most* important thing to you. Stop whining. Go do it.

I was twenty-four when I started Lead Concept. And back then, we didn't have seed money or GoFundMe, and we didn't have investors. We used our first check from our first client, and I still remember waiting for that check to arrive. In fact, I'm sure the first check just came to the apartment I was living in before we even opened up a post office box. That check came in, and it paid for the post office box, and the next check probably paid for the office rent, and then we got phones in the office. Each check that came in was applied to our startup costs, and a small commission was paid to the salesperson who brought that in. Because there were four of us, we had to earn an income. We had to pay our own bills at home. So, when calculating our bills, taxes, credit card fees, and commissions, I thought I had everything all figured out, but the truth is I didn't.

With each passing month, we were paying out more than we were bringing in, and it didn't take very long to figure out there was a problem there. It became apparent that the company we were running was in jeopardy. I remember standing on the balcony of my brother Steve's apartment. He's been working with me for thirty years now, standing up for me in tough times and supporting my good and bad choices along the way, but he wasn't working with me at the time. I was standing on the balcony of his apartment, looking out over the street and thinking, *I guess I have to get another job because I didn't do this one right.*

It seemed that the best way to deal with this issue was to face it straight on. I figured out the math that I needed to do better, and then I called all the vendors I was buying lists and paper and envelopes from and explained that I wouldn't be able to pay for them yet. I can tell you that they did not like hearing that I had no money because I had been miscalculating our overall costs and accidentally ran the bank account dry, but they were all thankful for my honesty. Rather than close my accounts, they agreed to put me on a cash-up-front payment system where I had to pay for any new goods I purchased when I ordered them. They also allowed me to pay back my old debts over time. It would take me over two years to pay off that debt, but I kept digging in to make those payments. As a result, my relationships with these people grew stronger because they now knew I would live up to my word. I was honest about the challenges that I was having at Lead Concepts, and my vendors were thankful for my honesty. Unfortunately, we aren't used to that in business.

In business and in life, many things happen to us that are setbacks. Thirty years later, some of those vendors are still my vendors. And I've had to have that conversation once or twice again since then because sometimes, that happens in business. But by focusing on what needed to be done and then looking forward instead of complaining about what had happened, I was able to find a solution.

My dad was the most driven and energetic businessman, father, husband, and teacher. He fought his way out of New York City. He fought in Golden Gloves matches. He always sent money to his mother, my Nanny. My parents gave me a lot, and I can only hope I did the same for my children. My father said that there will always be roadblocks, but they're just bumps in the road. If you're looking down, the bumps are going to seem bigger. Look forward, instead. Look at where you're going. The farther down the road you look, the tinier those bumps will seem in comparison.

Most people complain, and they seem to enjoy complaining. They complain about things that are within their control instead of fixing them. They also complain about things they can't control, and that's the worst. Think about what you want *most*. This is what will help you to solve a problem. Most of the things you worry about will never happen—so don't worry about them. I know that's easy to say and not so easy to do. And some people are built to worry more than others. If you're built to worry, that's fine, but don't let worry drive your decisions. Focus on the next steps toward what you really want *most*. Be aware of your fears, but don't let them slow you down. Then make a decision and move forward.

I never had a propensity to say, "Poor me," when something went wrong. When I found myself going through a divorce that I never thought would happen, I quickly determined that even though my home life was coming apart, it made little sense to let my work life do the same. By then, there would have been twenty to thirty people at the company. I spent hours at the office every day with these people. They had become my work family, friends, associates, and confidants. I knew what I wanted most at that moment was to be there for my children, Courtney, Jessica, and CJ. (CJ calls himself Christopher now, but if he indulges me, I'll refer to him as Christopher, Jr. or CJ throughout this book.) But I also knew that complaining about what I was going through wouldn't help (not that I didn't complain at all). I needed to focus first on what I wanted *most*—for the kids to have what they needed, to be able to make it to their games or practices, and to get them to school on time with homework done and lunches packed. I had to focus on being at home when I was at home, and then I could focus on being at work when I was at work. My brother Steve stepped up more than ever during these times and helped me run the business. He was the company's savior, and he certainly saved me at a time when I needed to focus on creating success at home. Not letting the business fall into disrepair was important because losing my income would only make things worse.

Of course, time passed, and eventually, life settled back down. The kids were either resilient or learned resilience as a result of our circumstances—and they got what they needed from Dad. I began to feel the work-life balance shift back to work because I thought that being a good earner during that time would make everything easier at home. It was a bump in the road for me personally, the biggest bump I ever faced. And while I'm sure I did think *Poor me,* I didn't say it out loud.

Take the time to ask yourself, at various times in your life, what do I want most? That question can change everything. It can help you make the biggest decisions in your life. Do I buy a new car? Do I buy a house? Do I buy stocks? Do I buy a new watch? Do I eat that piece of cake? What do you want *most* in life? If your decision goes against the things you believe are most important, then it's probably not the right decision. Ask yourself what really matters, what you want *most* from life, faith, and family. For me, there would be no bigger hardship or personal failure than if my family came apart. You'll want many things in life: faith, family, security, relationships, travel, money. If you're like me, you'll want to make sure your partner gets what they want *most* in life too, and your job is to help them get there. Ask your spouse or partner to go to a quiet place and consider what matters *most* to them. You may be surprised by what you both learn.

THREE
BE NICE NO MATTER WHAT

This seems like a simple concept you wouldn't have to write a chapter about, doesn't it? Why would I have to expand on the concept of being nice? Well, it sounds simple, but being nice can sometimes be challenging.

I had a client leave me a message one morning, and when I called him back some minutes later, he was mad at me because I didn't take his call, and he was happy to tell me that. But I've known this client for a while, and I explained that I had been on another call. I apologized but told him he had me now, and we could move forward and get his questions answered. He said he was sorry for getting so angry, but was concerned that the advertisement he was ordering from me would cost a lot of money. He was worried about losing his house and his wife if he didn't start making money. That moment was real and emotional, and I understood that he was upset, but I knew then that he wasn't upset with me. He was just upset at his current situation.

I talked with him for a few minutes, and once I settled him down, we moved on to talking about the advertisement that I would be preparing for him. He did end up having success, but it was likely due to his determination rather than anything I did on his mailing campaign. This man was a thoughtful, caring person, a nice, gentle soul, but money had him so stressed out that he said things he normally wouldn't. And that is often the case with people—if something is going on, whether a health issue or a money issue, they take it out on those around them.

There have been several times in the business that I've been running for thirty-three years now that I had more bills than I had money. And yes, it created stress for me, but I always focused on what we needed to do to fix the problem rather than dwelling on it or saying, "Poor me." I asked myself, *Now what do we do? If we need more revenue, how can we create it? Can we make more phone calls? Maybe create a new mailer to give me a reason to call all my clients?*

I found it better to be nice to my vendors and tell them the truth about my situation. In my experience, most people are not nice in these situations, and I'm not sure I blame them for that, but it often ends badly for them and doesn't help them get to where they want to be in life. I would rather be nice and save the relationship, whether it's personal or business. Who knows where this person will end up? They might end up working for me or vice versa. They might turn out to be a good friend you can talk to about life and business.

Being nice can be difficult when you encounter people who are not built the same way as you are. They may embrace the fact that they're not nice or simply not realize it. I often recognize this type of person and determine that it's better to keep my answers short and to the point. In cases like this, I am completely honest and professional in my responses, and I make sure to get paid for the job before I mail it.

Some people are just prone to having a bad day. Sometimes, the challenges of everyday life can weigh on people so much that they carry them around with them, and they can sometimes be rude to you. They complain to you or take it out on you. Imagine if, instead of getting emotional, you didn't push back. Instead of fighting back, you simply said, "Oh no, that's terrible," or "I'm sorry that happened to you."

I have seen this done many times by one of the most sympathetic people I know. Wendy was my assistant for years, but she eventually became a salesperson and now runs the sales and customer service department. She is responsible for more people at Lead Concepts than anyone else in the building. She taught me this, and although I can't possibly do it as well as she can, I certainly aspire to it. Wendy has a way of taking your bad mood or rude behavior and somehow absorbing it so you don't have it anymore. When you leave her office, you feel better because you left your issue or complaint behind. It took me some time to realize why everyone, including me, always wanted to talk to Wendy about their challenges. She simply accepted them and made you realize it was okay to feel that way without ever saying those words.

Being nice means taking a deep breath and realizing that, in most cases, people wake up every morning intending to do the best they can with that day. But then, sometime during the day, something happens that pushes them off course. Like when you're driving and someone speeds past you and maybe cuts you off, and you let that ruin your day. It's a choice you're making.

Some people deal with stress differently than others. I don't know how you deal with it, but hopefully, you'll take the time to think about it and consider the direction you're going. If you have worries about something that hasn't happened yet, keep in mind that it may never happen. I've always found that if I smile at someone or say something nice about their hair, shoes, or choice of dress for that day, it makes them feel good, and it always makes me feel good. But I think when you smile at someone, the hope is that they'll smile at someone else later.

Surrounding myself with people who are mean or rude to each other is not something I want to do. I want to spend time with people who are positive, people who are upbeat, people who are looking to the future, and people who speak nicely to each other. I think when you spend time with people who speak in a nasty way, you have to be careful because it might rub off on you a little bit. You have to choose the people that you're going to be in the room with and be nice no matter what. This means giving people grace to be who they are. Don't expect them to be the same as you. Some people will see the world in a completely different way than you do. My big brother Bill and I tend to see the world very differently. When he worked with me, I could always count on him to see things I didn't see. My brother is one of the nicest business people I know— he roots for everyone to be successful, and he will do anything he can to help you succeed, even if it's not in his best interest.

Being nice seems unnecessary until you start breaking down just how hard it can sometimes be to deal with rude or unreasonable people in business or in general. I can tell you that being nice is worth it and has served me well over many years. Be friendly but professional. I hope you find your balance.

FOUR
IT'S THE TOUGH THINGS THAT TEACH YOU

I don't know exactly when I figured this out. Because when you're young, everything seems hard. I remember being in elementary school, thinking it was hard, but when I got to middle school, I realized that elementary school was easy. I remember thinking high school was difficult, but then I went to college and realized high school was easy. Someone once told me about a brain surgeon coming out of surgery and saying it was easy. But that was because he had performed the same surgery many times and knew what he was doing, so it was easy for him. Repetition makes things easy.

You learn more about yourself when you're doing something difficult. At the age of forty, I knew I could run a marathon. I wasn't trying to win it, but I knew I could run it. I could, as I say, lean forward for 26.2 miles or four and a half hours. But it is difficult to train for that marathon and to plan every run and every meal for several months in preparation to put your body through the rigors of what would typically be between four to four and a half hours to run five miles, then eight miles, then three miles in preparation for a weekend where maybe you had to run sixteen or eighteen or twenty-two miles. That means your training runs now are three hours of stress on the body.

But when you get done with one of those long training runs, put in all the work you knew you needed to, brought food and water with you, and were able to replenish along the run, and when you got done with that training run, and you didn't hurt, you knew you'd be ready to in a few days. For me, three miles was very easy. I could lean forward for thirty minutes or so and be done. But when you're looking at the pavement, and you've been jogging for three or four hours, you learn a lot because it does hurt when you're running for that long. And when you're between eighteen and twenty-two miles, your body starts to shut down a little. You depend more on your will to continue. It's that will to succeed that I hope and desire for my children, grandchildren, and their children.

Willpower. You are working through tough times and seeing them through. Hurting—sometimes physically and sometimes emotionally—but not giving up. Instead, stay in it by thinking and using your heart and mind to continue past whatever it is.

When I lost my marriage, there was no time to say, "Poor me." I had three kids. You look at what matters the most in those times, and it helps you find perspective. From there, you find the willpower to look at what you need to do today instead of complaining about what happened to you yesterday. I don't know whether running a marathon helped me manage the loss of my family or just gave me the willpower to keep going. But there was happiness at the end of this part of my life when I found Kim.

I think I've always had a certain amount of willpower. But as I've aged, I have found that I no longer want to do things if they're easy. I lost interest. When I start doing something hard, it keeps me focused, and once I've done it enough, I get better at it. Then I get bored again and want to do something else. This often served me poorly until I learned to understand when to apply it and when to stick with something to achieve a higher goal.

Running my company for thirty-three years, chasing after those things that I thought were hard or interesting to me, and allowing myself to get bored, as I say, with other projects, wasn't conducive to running a strong company. I had to learn to manage what that meant. As I get older and lean into retirement, I hope to get back to doing more of those difficult things that challenge me. Growing up, I was never comfortable on the dance floor. Oh, I wanted to be out there because I never wanted to be stuck on the sidelines—I still don't—but I never felt like I was a good dancer. So, in my forties, I started taking dance lessons and realized I had to give myself some grace. I had to give myself permission to be bad at dancing until I could get good at it. I just needed somebody to show me where to put my feet. Turns out I was never bad at dancing at all. I just had someone telling me I was.

I hope that as you choose the things you will be doing with your life, you won't simply select the easiest things. There are a lot of other people doing that. I know that only a small percentage of people on the planet have ever run a marathon, let alone two, and in my case, eight. I was interested in doing marathons because I felt like most people wouldn't do it. But when you set out to do a marathon, and you see 30,000 other people standing in the cold with you, getting ready for the race to start, you start to think, *Well, maybe this isn't as unique as I thought.*

Of course, that's not true. It is, in fact, unique to run a marathon. But you can get swept away by the thought of 30,000 people running one somewhere in the country every weekend, and that's just in this country alone. So, I lost some interest in running marathons because it was now easy for me. And that is when I learned about a different kind of marathon called a "destination marathon." I didn't give it any thought at all—I knew I wanted to run a destination marathon called the Antarctic Ice Marathon.

The prospect of running a marathon in the freezing cold only a few miles from the bottom of the earth sounded difficult. It was hard enough to pique my interest. I signed up quickly, paid the sizable entry fee, and then waited to find out when I would get to go. I emailed the race organizer, who is from Galway, Ireland, and an "extreme athlete." I sent that email and waited a considerable number of days for a reply. I thought he might be busy or disorganized or simply didn't care, but when I did get that reply, he said, "Sorry for the delay in responding. I have been running across South America." He had literally been running thirty to forty miles every day from one side of South America at the Atlantic Ocean to the other side at the Pacific Ocean. He is one of the most unique people I have met.

As it turns out, my trip to Antarctica had little to do with the run itself, which was, in fact, the most challenging physical test I have endured. It was more about the location, the people I met, and the relationships I would find worldwide. From Minnesota and various parts of the US to the UK, Belgium, Poland, Russia, Australia, Mumbai, Japan, China, and Sri Lanka, we all lifted each other to get to the finish line. When it was time to leave the next morning on a Russian cargo plane, we were told we would be stuck there for several days due to bad weather in South America. We would spend the next three extra days growing together and bonding as a group. Our families back home were all worried, but we were more than fine.

Getting to this event was difficult, and running the race was incredibly hard, but it did show me just how much willpower I have. It's a reminder that marathoning, dancing, training runs, and doing the difficult things are what teach us the most. These are opportunities to learn something about yourself. I didn't want to be on the sidelines watching. I wanted to be in the game. I hope you'll want to be in the game, as I did. Keep learning to dance, or play piano, or strum the guitar.

Only eighteen months ago, I found out my company was in debt of nearly 2.5 million dollars. It got me focused, got me in the game of running my company every day, lifting up the people around me, and letting my vendors know of our financial challenges. When I called those vendors, they were not nice, and I understood why. I stayed nice no matter what when talking to them and promised that we would certainly get our bills paid. It took willpower and consistency, but the company did it. *We* did it, and *we* made it through. Everyone learned more about themselves in that time. Several times, I got up in front of everyone at the company and explained where we were, why we were there, and how we were going to get out of debt.

During this time, I realized I wasn't as good as I wanted to be at speaking in front of people. So I started doing it every chance I got, getting up in front of people to speak. I wasn't great at it when I started, but I think I am now. I'm comfortable. I enjoy it. I would get very nervous before getting on stage to do my public speaking. Sometimes I want to change my message and tell people something easier to say, rather than something new, different, positive, or uplifting. More than once, I almost didn't get on stage, but I made myself do it and gave myself permission to be bad. I wasn't bad, but I didn't know if I would be good. If you're intentional about what you do in life, you don't always have to pick the toughest path. I'm just hoping you won't always choose the easiest path.

Maybe Pop's only attempted poem will help you understand.

Fear

Fear is real, but doers do
Fear is real, but logic pushes it aside
Failure is required to live life full
Doers do, knowing failure lingers inside
When fear prevents action, life is null

Fear will not dull my light
My light must shine bright
The assumption of yes I require
To create action that one day will inspire

Fear is real, but I set it aside
I will grow without fear to fail
I grab every chance to reach outside
To grow is my true grail

My only limit is put on myself
Fear of failure is tough to resist
The assumption of NO exists
The only option to push it off itself

Fear is real
Logic must prevail
Or it will prevent my next inhale
Fear is real, but doers do

Your Pop is a confident person, but adding this to my story was very difficult to do as I don't think it's very good. I do think it says what I want you to hear, though. You can be afraid—that's normal—but when you apply logical thought to it, you will see you have no choice but to push past the fear and do it anyway.

FIVE
IF YOU DON'T LIKE WHAT YOU'RE DOING, SO WHAT?

Because of my level of success—and my advanced age, I suppose—young people often ask for my time and want to talk to me about success or life or maybe just ask for my guidance about the direction they're heading in. About two years ago, I had an unusual conversation with a guy who wanted to ask me some questions. He was about thirty-five and was married with two young children. He'd been working for a company and said, "I didn't like the job I was doing. I liked the company, and I liked the company culture, but I didn't like my role there." To his credit, he made the decision to move on and took a position with a different company. Here's where the story gets interesting. Of his new company, he said, "I love what I'm doing now, but I don't like the company. I don't care for the owner, and I don't like the culture there." I asked him if he was making a good living, and he said he was making over six figures, meaning more than $100,000 a year. He was doing well—making a six-figure income at thirty-five is impressive, and it was enough to support his family. But it seemed to me that he could find something he didn't like in just about anything. With the first job, he didn't like what he was doing, but he liked the company. With the second, he liked what he was doing but didn't like the company. It made me wonder if he just didn't like working.

I reminded him that his real job in life was to be there for his family financially. Obviously, he also had to be there emotionally, but he could do that while still having a good income, whether he thought it was a good job or a good company. I'm assuming that whatever work he was doing was viable and, of course, legal. If he is working with a legitimate business with a strong foundation and the potential to move up in the company, then his real job becomes creating financial stability for his family. Even better, if his role allows him to learn a trade or helps him create his own business and eventually use his knowledge to become self-employed, he can create vast wealth for his family down the road.

Even at a young age, I knew I wanted to make money. Whatever I chose to do, I wanted there to be no limit on my income. Wherever I worked, I was determined to be the best at what I did. I would rather choose something to do and decide to like it than choose to do what I like and not have the income potential associated with it. If you're working and decide to like what you do, you'll find joy in whatever it is you're doing. If you're like me, you hope to bring joy to the people you work with. The more I could do at work, the less somebody else had to do. If you're going to work—and it's likely you'll have to—I suggest you choose something where you can make good money and then make it fun. Make it something you can learn and, over time, have the option of going out on your own to do it. You don't *have* to go on your own, but it's always nice to have that option. You don't have to agree with me now, but you might when you get older.

I always knew I wanted to own my own business. I knew I wanted to run my own business because I wanted to be able to make as much money as possible. And I was going to find joy in whatever I was doing as long as there was an opportunity for me to really make big money. Over the years, there have been some years where we did really well and some years where we did not. Today, I find more joy in helping others make more money than in making more myself.

I believe anybody who can work should work. And learn to make it fun and joyful—wherever you may be. Why not choose a job, a profession, or even start your own business where you can lift up others around you along the way? Make the day just a little bit brighter for others when you walk through the door.

The money we make should be used to lift up the lives of the people we come into contact with. Yes, it'll touch your family first. Tipping a waiter more than usual not only helps them but also brings me joy. When I see homeless people, I go to the ATM and get $20 bills and give one to each person when I pass by. I don't know if it helps them overall, but it will at least help them for a few minutes—and it makes me feel good. Choose a couple of charities and donate. I'm passionate about homeless shelters, but you can be passionate about whatever charity you'd like. Imagine a time in your financial life when you can give back that way. You will find so much joy.

SIX
SEEK IMPROVEMENT EVERYWHERE AND IN ALL THINGS

My father was the most competitive person many people knew. And he always said it was good to be competitive. I believed in that and leaned into that—I competed hard in everything I did. In competition, you learn to win with grace and lose with grace. Don't be happy that you lost. Don't be content that you lost. But when it's done, and you have, in fact, lost whatever the competition was, just shake hands and practice more.

In my youth, competition meant that somebody wins and somebody loses. And that's true today and will likely be forever. But when you reach a certain age in adulthood, your competitive tendencies have to change because you reach a point where you're competing with yourself and nobody else. You are looking at who you are today and how you can be better tomorrow—not better than someone else, just better. This is something I'm obsessive about and have been for fifteen years. As I mentioned before, I was running four to four-and-a-half-hour marathons. Of course, there were people running them in two and a half hours. Much, much faster than me. I could never compete with somebody running that much faster than me. Nor was it important that I do so. What I wanted to do was be a little bit faster next time (which, by the way, I'm not sure I ever did, even though I tried).

As a youngster, I was very slender. I always jokingly said, "Chris was built for speed, not power." I was 165 or 170 pounds and looked like I could barely defend myself. So, I started lifting and eating. What type of training do I need to do? What kind of diet do I need to follow? What should my weight be? There was always somebody lifting more than me in the gym, and they had probably been doing it longer than me. I couldn't compete with them, and it wasn't important to compete with them. I was competing with only myself—to be fitter, bigger, faster, and to increase my VO2 max so I could run faster or longer.

Of course, there were a lot of resources out there to help me with my fitness objectives. And those same resources are available for every topic. I wanted to be better at *everything*. I wanted to be a better spouse, a better husband, a better boss, and a better parent. I wanted to learn to be more patient. If you can find a book you like and a mentor you like, those are the things that will shape you. Author and motivational speaker Zig Ziglar said, "You are who you are and what you are because of what has gone in your mind," so put good stuff in your mind. Whether it's a book, a podcast, a video, a movie, a documentary, or the people you spend time with. Remember, if you spend time with people who are nasty to each other, you may find yourself accidentally slipping into that mindset. Don't spend time with people who put negative thoughts in your head. Make sure you always stay positive.

I've always had lofty financial goals. I'm not competing with anyone—only with myself. Am I a little bit better this year than last year? Write down all of your bills, credit card payments, and car payments at the beginning of the year, and then write them all down again at the end of the year and see if they're smaller. If your bills and debts are growing, maybe you're doing something wrong. But guess what? There are a vast number of books and resources on financial goals. I've read and listened to just about every one of them. Just remember, whether you read a book or listen to a mentor, you have to decide whether it makes sense to you. Growth doesn't happen by simply believing or agreeing with all the information you gather. When you put those thoughts in your mind and then think about what makes sense in your life or doesn't, that's when growth occurs.

If you take the time to do that, you'll learn the difference between good debt and bad debt.

You'll learn about the "Rule of 72" in investing—dividing 72 by the annual rate of return gives investors a rough estimate of how many years it will take for the initial investment to duplicate itself. The "Rule of 72" is a simple way to determine how long an investment will take to double, given a fixed annual rate of return.

If you've taken some of these chapters to heart and are choosing to move into a field where you're going to both find joy and make as much money as you can, you need to learn what to do with that extra money. Of course, you're going to give some of it away to the people and charities around you. But learning how to invest your money properly, whatever that means to you, will serve you well over time. I'll leave it up to you to read about those things.

As a young person, you're learning to compete, but you're competing against other people. But as an adult, are you competing with yourself every quarter and every year, tracking your own progress and keeping tabs on how you're doing? And what are you doing as a spouse, father, investor, and money manager? Have you learned something today or put something in your mind that will prepare you for tomorrow? Striving to be better every day is hard to do, but I hope you make the decision to do what it takes to better yourself.

SEVEN
STAND OUT FROM THE CROWD

Stand out from the crowd by finding a different way to do things. In Chapter 1, I discussed the need to recruit employees to my company. The results weren't there when I mindlessly placed ads that looked just like everybody else's. But when I completely changed my ad to stand out from the crowd, it brought immense results. I'm not trying to say that you should always be doing something different from everyone else, but I would ask you, my children, grandchildren, and great-great-grandchildren, to be intentional. It's okay to go along with the crowd if you've looked at it and thought about it, and it makes sense.

In my lifetime, I've participated in some swimming events. It's been found that swimmers who swim in a row create a wake and swim so much faster, following one behind the other. Even if that group took a longer journey to get from point A to point B, if you took a direct line to swim, it would take you longer because you don't have the wake to swim in. So even though the path is shorter, it could take you just as long or longer to get there. So, be intentional with your decision-making when it comes to the crowd. Take a look at what everyone else is doing. Instead of just doing it, ask questions. Take a look at the easy path, and if that's where everyone is going and you want to go that way, then go. But don't just follow them without asking yourself if that is the best way for you. You aren't like most of them—and I say that with confidence because you have learned to look and think. You have learned what is called "critical thinking," the kind of thinking in which you question, analyze, and evaluate to make a judgment about what you read, hear, or experience. As a reminder from Pop, good critical thinking doesn't mean being negative or focusing on faults. It means clarifying your thinking so that you can make better-informed decisions. Science says that no one is born with these skills—they are learned and improved with practice. So, keep practicing and learn to have a critical-thinking mindset.

Perhaps all your friends want to attend the same college. You want to join them, but maybe it's not the best college for you, your future, or your path. Whether to follow your buddy or not is a question I hope you will always be asking yourself, and it's a metaphor for many different things related to getting from point A to point B.

When I'm in the airport, I've noticed that most people take the escalator up or down rather than the stairs. I find the stairs are usually faster. As my kids know, I always make sure it's faster. Considering how much money I have spent over the years on fitness and health, why would I stand still on the escalator when I can walk down the stairs? Why is everyone rolling their suitcases when we used to carry them? I sometimes carry my suitcase up or down the stairs because I'm exercising at the same time. I think my way is better.

When you go to school, and everyone's wearing the same brand of clothing, ask yourself, *Do I want to dress like everyone else?* And know that it's perfectly okay to dress like everyone else. If you want to fit in, that's normal. But if you want to dress just like them, I want you to be intentional about it. Look at what they're wearing, and wear basically the same thing, but maybe try to look a little bit nicer—fix your hair, make sure you're ready for your day, and if you have to wear a baseball cap, wear it straight. I don't know what straight means to you because I'm older, and straight just simply means facing forward, but for you, maybe it's backward.

At the time of writing this book, mustaches weren't considered fashionable, but I've just learned that younger men are trying to bring them back into fashion. At my age, a mustache is still not in fashion. So you might think, *Well, then Pop must be wearing a mustache.* But in this case, I've thought about it, and standing out from the crowd by wearing a mustache isn't what I want to do—so I am *intentionally* following the crowd by not wearing a mustache. I often have a beard, which, unfortunately, is 60 to 70 percent gray, but that's okay because I look my age.

For me, standing out from the crowd might include dressing up differently than others. For instance, I've gone to marketing meetings and events where I tried to stand out from the crowd by the way I dress. As far as you are concerned, my children and grandchildren, I think you already stand out from the crowd.

Look at what others are doing and ask yourself if that's really the best way to do it. Often, you will discover it's not. It's not because you're trying to be right or to prove someone wrong. You're simply looking for a different and better way to think about something. I know in my business, every time I think we've got something exactly right, it turns out there's a better way. We must keep looking and asking questions until we find our new, better way.

EIGHT
TAKE PEOPLE WITH YOU ON YOUR JOURNEY

I'm a people person. I enjoy meeting people from all different places and backgrounds. The best way to meet people is to ask them questions about themselves. Most people like to talk about themselves and what is going on in their lives, good or bad. If you're curious about them, ask good questions. You will frequently find out you have the same challenges or hobbies. Once you find a common interest, conversation becomes easier. You might find a person to train for a marathon with or a partner to share your life.

Taking people with you on your journey means even more when talking about business. When you find great people to work with you in business, as I have been lucky to do, you'll find that the journey is more fun, and you get where you're going faster.

This is never truer than when I'm riding my road bike with a group. This is an easy analogy for a cyclist. When riding a road bike, the bigger group you have, the faster you're going—the strongest ride in the front, and the weakest fall into the wake and get pulled along. I've seen people in business who do everything themselves. They hire people if they feel like they have to, but they don't want to break free of the few dollars it costs because they either want to keep all the money for themselves or can't trust someone else to do the work. I've coached people on the topic of delegating work, so I understand the lack of trust involved. If you don't trust that the work will be done correctly, you either have not trained this person enough or need to find someone you can trust.

In doing all of the work yourself, your business never evolves. It never grows. And if it's not growing, it's dying. You can only go so far by yourself; if you have intentionally determined to do so, that's okay, but I'd say it's short-term thinking. It's the easy way out. It's an easy way out because hiring can be so difficult.

Since I've always had an incredibly positive attitude toward life and people, it seemed like it was easier for me to find great people. As with that newspaper ad that generated so many good interviews, we found more great people than we needed to hire. And if they were great, we hired them anyway. If your hire doesn't work, for whatever reason, shake hands and wish them well. However, don't give up looking for people to join your company who are positive, uplifting, and looking to learn and grow. Your company will grow if these people are able to ask questions and do things differently, not just to be different, but to make sure the way you're going is the right way.

When someone who's been with me for years decides it's time to go, it's never a surprise because it was always my objective for them to come and stay for a period of time, grow, learn, evolve, and then move on to bigger goals. Hopefully, they can find more success, make more money, and be fulfilled. We never want the people who work with us to leave, but we know when we find the good or the great ones, there is a chance, often a big chance, that they will eventually go. They're looking to improve all the time, so when they outgrow the company and it's time for them to move on, you applaud them and wish them well. It's no different from when a client decides they need to move in a different direction or do some other form of marketing that doesn't include us. Our clients have to make the best business decision they can make for themselves, and if it doesn't include us today, it doesn't mean it won't include us later. Some will come back, and some will not. But why not be nice regardless? I wish them well and root for their success because they're on a journey, too.

The need for a business to grow and adapt has shown itself to me many times over the years, but never as clearly as in the last two years. While I traveled to see my customers and ask questions about the products they were selling, I found that the market was changing. My company was making more money than it ever had, but that money was going back into our future growth—hiring salespeople with different skills than our current in-house team, developing new products, and traveling around the country to establish personal relationships with our customers. But while my company was making so much money, so were several of my competitors. These companies have been competitors of mine for all the thirty-plus years I have been in business. But in nearly all of my travels, they were not there. They weren't meeting the customers face to face where they live, and they weren't adapting to the changes I could see coming. They were making money and not reinvesting. They were taking the easy path. They were not trying to grow. As I've said already, a business that isn't growing is dying, and now, all three of my major competitors are barely existing.

With almost fifty people now who like coming to work and lifting each other up, our company is on a journey and moving faster than ever. The challenge as my company grows—and one day, this will be your challenge—is to come to work every day ready to do the work and lift everybody up along the way. It's not challenging for me because I like it. It's part of me. It's who I am. I hope the people working there can see that I like it, that I smile at them and laugh with them. And when we find out we're in debt, we work our way out of it together. Our company is asking the right questions, being intentional, and working together, and we're always looking for great people who want to join in on our journey. You may have to hire two people to find one great one. You may have to hire four people to find one great one. But doing the work all on your own is short-term thinking.

You may make more money in the short term if it's only you, but the longer the business runs, the more money you will make in the long term. The more money you make, the more you're managing to grow. And when I consider the people I work with today on our payroll and how it affects them, their families, their parents, the people around them, and their communities, they're all on their own journey at home, while at the same time on one with us at the office. I'll spend more time today and tomorrow talking to my team members about their journey at home. I think maybe I haven't been doing that enough.

NINE
WORK-LIFE BALANCE

There has to be a work-life balance, but that balance can be different for everyone. For some people, family first might mean 35 percent of the time, and for others, it could be 65 percent. Many people say you shouldn't put work first. They don't want to work so hard that they don't get to see their family. My father was a tireless family man and a fantastic critical thinker. He traveled for work most weeks but rarely over the weekend, and when he was with us, we felt his love and pride for us. Even though he was working a lot, I always felt him there.

When I started Lead Concepts at the age of twenty-four (that would have been in October 1991), the apartment I lived in was right behind the building where I rented space for our first office. I often had trouble sleeping because the company was just getting started. There was nothing there, and we needed an office, phones, a computer, and a typewriter—yes, I said a typewriter. To say that, at that time, I had a work-life balance of 50-50 would be silly because I'd guess that getting the business started required 90 percent of my energy. However, I wasn't married, and I didn't have children, so even though I was working or thinking about work all the time, it didn't create an imbalance. When people talk about work-life balance—and I have heard and seen it a lot on "The Gram" as young people call Instagram (this joke is for my kids) and on social media—people mistakenly act like the balance should lean heavily toward family time, but if you're not making enough money, then that is not valid to me. Fifty percent to home and the other fifty to work is the perfect scenario, but in my opinion, it's often unrealistic.

If you are working for somebody else, it might be okay to commit 50 percent to work and 50 percent to home—you might not move up in the company very quickly, but that's not always true. But when you're working in a business, you might be required to give more than 50 percent. If the company you're working for begins to falter, it may require you to step up and give 70 or 80 percent of your time. That can be exceedingly difficult if you're married with children and managing all of the kids' schedules or if you have someone in your home who is sick. And in difficult times at work, the balance might have to lean toward work.

Similarly, when trying times occur at home, the balance may shift back to home. Neither one is right or wrong. In my thirty-three years at Lead Concepts, things have changed, rules have changed, government regulations have changed, and if the products we were mailing weren't working, we had to look for something different. At times, the company needed me to give 70, 80, or 90 percent. But I learned that if I communicated that to the people in my life, they would understand. In my case, I often ask for permission from my family to give more attention to work for the time being.

Hopefully, the shift in balance is a short-term change. What you want to be careful of, though, is working a lot but not being organized enough to make the time you spend at work productive. I've seen a lot of people who are very, very busy all the time but seem to accomplish very little. Guess what? There are books to help you with time management. There are podcasts on this subject. You can absolutely study that, get more organized, and identify ways to make sure that the time you spend at work is prioritized on the things that matter most on that day. That way, when you go to work, you know the two or three most important things you need to accomplish on that day, and you can get them done so that when you go home, you can emotionally disengage from work. You'll know that you didn't just go to work and put in eight hours for nothing. You went to work, and you got the things accomplished that you needed to accomplish. When you plan and organize your day the night before work and feel like you had a productive day at the office, you can go home at the end of the day and focus on your home, spouse, and kids and not think about work. The hope is that you finish the things you need to at work, and you don't have to bring them home with you either physically or emotionally. And if you have an off day, which happens sometimes, reset for tomorrow. Don't be too hard on yourself. Tomorrow will be better.

When I was a young man, I often felt guilty at home that I wasn't working more, and when I went to work, I felt guilty that I wasn't at home with the kids. That's no way to live. It should be the exact opposite—don't feel guilty at home, and don't feel guilty at work. Give your attention and focus to each half of that work-life balance and communicate it with the people at home and at the office. If you have something big happening at home, someone is sick, or someone needs attention… Well, it helps if you communicate that at the office. So often, it's honest and open communication that solves the problem. Let the people in your world know about what's happening because they want to create success for you just as you do for them (remember what I said earlier—I like everyone and assume they want the best for everyone). I mentioned earlier that when I have financial challenges at the office and I might be unable to pay a bill or a creditor, I call and communicate that to them. That communication is always appreciated, and it's the same thing whether you're running a business or a household.

Remember, everyone is different, so you are not wrong in how you balance things out. But do yourself a favor and communicate with the people you love and the people you count on at work when your work-life balance is about to go out of balance. Be intentional.

TEN
IF YOU'RE GOING TO DO ANYTHING, DO IT ALL THE WAY

"I have this great idea," I said. "I want to write a book for my kids and the generations to come." It was a crazy idea. I thought it would be hard to do, and it has been harder than I thought. But I prefer doing things that are hard, so it fits in perfectly with who I want to be. This is my favorite chapter to write for my kids, grandkids, and great-grandkids.

Hopefully, you will understand that the effort you put into everything you do will provide you with a huge advantage. If you put in the time to practice or study—anything from sports to the arts to salesmanship or managing money—then you will excel. The harder it is to do, the more time it will take to learn. You will learn more by doing the hard things, but you will learn nothing when doing something easy. I hope you learn to think bigger, better, and broader and realize that you *can* do it. I hope you will ask questions and learn about people instead of judging those around you. When you find the best people, the people who think like this, the people who do the hard things, spend time with those people. They will support you and lift you up. Being in their company will teach you more and help you to see things you might not have seen before.

Adrian Thomas is someone I want to spend as much time with as possible. He is always positive and thoughtful. He's inquisitive, never judges, and always asks good questions. One specific time that we were together, we talked about the company he runs. At the time, his company was making a profit of $1 million per month. Now, my company has been profitable most years, but never that profitable, and never profitable over several years in a row. This might sound crazy to some big businesspeople, but it's the truth. When I heard that Adrian's company was profitable at $1 million per month, I realized that my company had never been profitable. I didn't make $1 million per year, let alone per month. But at that moment, my eyes were opened to greater possibilities than I had ever seen before. Could I make my company profitable at $1 million per year and, even better, at $1 million per month?

That seemed really hard to do, but I chased after that goal, and two years later, we saw a profit of $2 million in one year. The trick was to sustain that and grow from there. I thought I was doing big things, but to increase my goals, I needed to spend even more time around people with bigger goals and thoughts than I did.

Thinking big and doing big things is about looking into the distance to see where you are going, instead of looking in the here and now at what other people are doing or not doing.

Planning your future by choosing what you want to do, where you want to go, and how fast you can get there is living your life with intent. I know people who go through life and let things happen to them instead of making things happen. I always want to be intentional about what I do and where I want to go.

At about the age of forty, I chose to do marathons, not half marathons, because, as I often tell people, why would I do anything that starts with the word half? My father taught me never to do things halfway.

When I was a young man, I started drinking red wine—not just any wine, but red wine. I didn't like it at first, but I had been underweight most of my life, and I discovered if I drank red wine with dinner instead of a Coke, I could eat more. You see, the bubbles in the Coke made me feel full faster, but when I drank red wine instead, I could eat more and gain a little weight. It might have been a silly reason to get started with wine, but that's how it happened. Once I learned to like it and read about wines from around the world, I began to collect some amazing red wines. I figured if I like it, I might as well have a refrigerated wine cellar with thousands of bottles of wine in it.

As youngsters, we drink coffee with milk. But adults and grown-ups often don't add milk to theirs. I started drinking coffee in college, but I wanted to drink it black, which took some getting used to. I eventually learned to like my coffee without any milk. I don't know when I went from drinking coffee to needing coffee. I guess I don't really need it, but I like it, and enough studies show that as long as you don't drink too much, it can have health benefits. I drink coffee every day, and although it took me until later in life, I realized if I was going to drink so much coffee, I could buy raw coffee beans and learn to roast them myself. I'm not sure what it is in my personality that once I think of something, I want to do it, to learn about it, and do it bigger than anyone else, or simply do things that others might not.

My father gave me so much good advice, and I give him credit for this. He said, "You can do any job you like, or you can like any job you do. And if you can make an excellent income at a job, why not learn to like that one?" I don't know if he would have remembered saying that, but it changed how I saw things. It was apparent to me at a young age that, with my personality, I should work for myself. I had a hard time taking instructions, especially from people I didn't think knew what they were talking about. As a teenager, I had an innate ability to listen to someone and decide whether I agreed with them or not. I wouldn't simply agree with someone because they were older than me or had a degree in some specialty. I was never intentionally disrespectful, but if what someone said did not make sense to me, then I was no longer interested in listening.

Even at the age of fifty, my personality test says, "Chris (*that's your Pop's name*) is good at following the rules." When I read that, I thought, *Okay, good. I've finally grown up. I'm fifty, and I am now ready to follow the rules.* But when I read the next sentence, a grin spread across my face: "Chris is good at following the rules, but only if he made them." Then I thought, *Oh Lord, I'm never going to change.* Who you are is who you are. You can act differently and pretend to be somebody different, but underneath it all, you are who you are.

For me, it was important that I start a business and make the rules. I have come to work every day for thirty-three years, and I'm still listening to podcasts, roasting coffee, collecting wine, going to conferences, and discovering that there is more to learn. There are forty-eight people working at Lead Concepts today, and I get the pleasure of seeing all of them most days. I hire them, and I pay them. I make sure they earn a good living. We work together toward that end, all of us. And that gets back to communication.

As I write this today, I'm fifty-six. My business could have been two or three times bigger if I had allowed myself to think bigger when I was twenty-four. But the company now, after thirty-three years, is slated for massive growth because I can now see the future. I can see the bigger opportunity to take the company from a direct mail advertising company limited to the confines of the United States Postal Service to an international digital marketing company specializing in lead generation in the direct mail and Facebook world for multiple markets. And that's just the beginning.

When you look at something that you want to do—and this will be difficult—ask yourself what it could be in ten years, twenty years, thirty years, forty years. As a young person, I wasn't able to do that. I don't know if you'll be able to do that either. But after reading these words, I hope you can get to that spot sooner than I was able to. Since I spent a lot of time at work, I created a wonderful life inside the world of Lead

Concepts. I've had a great career and still expect to be doing this for a while. And how lucky am I that Courtney, Jessica, and Christopher are all working here? I get to work with my brother, Steve. My mom, Lucy, your great-grandmother, comes to the office every day. Work-life balance—I brought my life to work, and I get to see everybody, the whole family, every day. I saw that possibility and knew I could create it many, many years ago. That's what I've always wanted *most* in life. Running a business may not be right for you. That's okay. You can still be your best at whatever you're doing. That's the most we can all ask for.

Put in the effort to learn, grow, and ask questions, and don't worry about what other people are doing or if they're growing faster than you or earning more money than you. That doesn't matter. The only thing that matters is that you're doing a little bit more, a little bit better each year, and hopefully lifting up the people around you along the way.

ELEVEN
GIVE BACK TO EVERYONE YOU CAN

Nothing will give you more joy than giving. Giving can mean giving time or energy or simply lending an ear and listening. For the sake of this chapter, however, we're talking about giving in a way that leans into money. We're talking about earning and how it affects the people around you.

I've said this before in this book—I believe that if you can work, you should work. I think I'll be able to work for many more years, but at some point, that could change. You never know when you might not be able to work anymore due to illness or an accident, so get to work now and start earning. When I hire people, I like to make sure they're making enough money to live appropriately. If I have people working for me who aren't making enough money to pay their bills, they'll be focused on surviving and trying to figure out how to pay their bills instead of their work. People have to make a proper living wage and then some. So that's certainly where I start with my giving.

When I talk about giving money, that's exactly what I mean. It's *giving* the money, not *loaning* the money. I have given tens of thousands of dollars away over the years, and I never ask for it back. That's the fastest way to lose a relationship. If you don't have the money to give, that's okay. Don't give it. When I give, I never think about that money again. Sometimes, distant relatives or friends have come to me in a time of need. I might give money to my kids or help somebody pay their mortgage. I'm giving to them and lifting them up, but I'm also giving myself joy. It brings me happiness to be able to gift that money to them.

When I was a young adult and starting my business, I was hoping to buy my first house, which required a 20 percent down payment. My first home cost $124,000, so that down payment would cost me $24,800. I had the money for the down payment, but I had also accumulated $10,000 in credit card debt in my brief time as an adult, and that credit card debt was getting in the way of my qualifying for the house. I had to ask my grandmother for help. She gave me the money to pay off those credit cards, which helped me get my first home. I remember having to ask my grandmother for that money. I wasn't proud of that. It was a lot of money for her. I felt lucky she was there to help me but disappointed in myself for mishandling my credit cards. It was a lesson about debt I'll never forget.

My father always wanted to give me money and tried to help me many, many times over the years. He would always ask if I needed any "help," as he called it, meaning money. He'd pull a $100 bill from his pocket and try to push it into my hand. He was always trying to help my brothers and me.

I will tell this story for the benefit of my two brothers, Bill and Steve, although I don't think Dad would have wanted it told. Later in his life, Dad told me that it gave him a lot of joy to be able to give money to his children. He confided in me that his father had given him a quarter in his lifetime—and he had done that to get him to go away. As my brothers know, Dad's father, George, was a transient figure in his life and would show up periodically to see his mother, Ruth, whom we affectionately call Nanny. George had come to the park to see Nanny, and in an effort to speak to Nanny alone, George gave my father twenty-five cents to go away and get some ice cream. It hurt my father to tell me that story, and as I write this, I find myself deeply saddened all over again for a man who could not have been a better husband and father to us all.

We are only talking about giving money, which is shortsighted because giving time is often more valuable than money. But I'm sure by now, you understand why I have limited this chapter to the money part of giving, and that is because you are already giving your time to the people who are most important to you. I know you are listening to their challenges without judging them or giving them advice on how to correct things. You are just listening, and that means so much more.

If there is one thing I would do better as the kids were growing up, and still now, it would be to give back to them more in listening. My wife, Kim, is an exceptional person and a great example of how I can do better at this. She will often provide valuable feedback on how I might have done better with my listening skills, and although it may not always seem like it to her, I listen and hope to apply her advice more often so I can be more like her. I give time to my kids because they are my priority, and I love them. I don't know that I always give them my ear, but I aspire to. I aspire to lift them up and give back to them more than just financially, but I'm still learning and growing. I can still do better.

TWELVE
HEAL YOURSELF WITH YOUR MIND

This is a statement that I have often made. And no, I don't think you can cure yourself of cancer or other terrible illnesses just by thinking them away. But I absolutely believe in and have practiced this concept many times in many situations with great success. I am positive that you are who and what you are because of what you put in your mind. Please note that I heard that while listening to the Zig Ziglar audio cassette of *See You at the Top*. He believed—and I agree—that if you're tired and keep telling yourself you're tired, then you *will* be tired. I'm not saying you can't be tired—what I'm saying is that if you are feeling tired, you could get up, drink some cold water, or go for a walk or a run to wake yourself up.

When you are on that walk, tell yourself, "I have so much energy," "I feel great," "My legs feel light, my lungs are full of air, and I could walk forever."

Don't say, "I don't feel tired," but say instead, "I feel energized. I feel ready for a big day."

The positive spin you put on the words you say to yourself will convince your brain that you are full of energy and propel you out of the cycle of being tired. I have done this many times while running marathons, and it absolutely works.

If you have seasonal allergies and the weather report says the pollen is high today, and you go outside expecting to be affected by the pollen, then you will be affected by the pollen. You'll walk outside and start sneezing, and your eyes will get red and itchy. But if you know that the pollen count is high today, you can put an allergy eye drop in each eye, start your car remotely, start the air conditioning early, and set yourself up for success. You'll go outside, knowing that the pollen can't beat you.

I have a cousin who is a thoughtful, wonderful, and loving person, but he has convinced himself that he is sick. His parents, aunts, uncles, sister, and cousins have all tried to convince him that he is okay. When I spend time with him, he is delightful, humorous, and quick with his wit and charm. In all ways, he is ready to participate in society, but he has convinced himself that he's unwell. In the quiet moments of his life, he tells himself he is sick. Until he finds a way to put something different and more positive in his mind, his mind will always remind him that he is sick.

You can be sick, sad, mad, or frustrated, and that's normal, but with knowledge and practice, you can choose not to let these things become who you are. It is often said, "If you *think you can* or *think you cannot*, you are probably right." I believe this is the most important message I can give you.

Pop's Recommended Reading For You Kids

As I mentioned earlier, you can find information in many ways, but I recommend that you read or listen to these books to put this information in your brain.

The Little Store on the Corner by Alice P. Miller

This is one of my very favorite children's books. It's the story of a small local store run by an owner who understands the concept of giving people more than they expect. His college-educated son pitches in to run the store for a while so that his dad can take a much-needed vacation, and he realizes the store can be more profitable if he gives away fewer peanuts, less candy, smaller scoops of ice cream and stops giving away free balloons. These changes were meant to make the store more profitable, and it was—until the customers decided to stop coming. This is a valuable lesson for every business owner.

See You at the Top by Zig Ziglar

This book crystallized for me the things that my parents instilled in me. My father lived a life of positive reinforcement. The idea that anything you do in life is easier if you take on that project with a positive mindset. If you believe you can achieve it, you will have a better chance of achieving it. Zig Ziglar's most famous and often-quoted statement, "You can have everything in life you want if you will just help other people get what they want," clarified how I was already thinking. I don't believe I could have said it as well as Zig, but it agreed with who I was and wanted to be. We live in a negative world, and you will be surrounded by negative people, but you can leave that negativity where you found it and not carry it with you for the rest of your day. The things that happen to you or for you can be taken in a positive light or a negative light. You get to decide. But don't take my word for it. Read the book, and you'll learn more about how your Pop and his father tried to live.

Ruthie's Kids: Tough Love From a Tough Mom by Bob Weir

This truly amazing story is about my father, who did not grow up with a father to teach him what he taught me. This book is called *Ruthie's Kids* by Dad's brother and my uncle. If you want to know how my father and his mom grew up, you can read that next. It's the true story of seven kids being raised by a single mother and talks about how my father grew up in absolute poverty in New York City in the '40s and '50s.

Who Moved My Cheese? by Dr. Spencer Johnson

This easy-to-read story perfectly illustrates how important it is to embrace change. It shows that when change comes, you can accept it, or you can die. And change is exactly what so many businesses—like Blockbuster or Sears or many others today that are fighting to stay afloat against the likes of online stores—fail to embrace.

The Richest Man in Babylon by **George S. Clason**

This is an inspirational story of a young man who learns the value of putting money away. He discovers that you can become incredibly wealthy by consistently spending less than you make and doing the right things with your money. It seems simple, but most cannot do it.

Rich Dad Poor Dad by **Robert Kiyosaki**

A business book written as a story or an autobiography of the life of a young boy growing up with his father and his best friend's father, each of whom has a totally different view of money. *Rich Dad Poor Dad* will help you clearly see what is an asset and what is a liability. The best part of this book is that it debunks the myth that a house is an asset. I can certainly tell you that my house constantly costs me money. Money that I could be investing in a much better place.

Blue Ocean Strategy by **W. Chan Kim and Renée Mauborgne**

The Blue Ocean Strategy is a simple concept to understand but quite challenging to achieve. A challenge that is most certainly worth the time and effort. The concept is to take what you are doing now that has so many competitors and place your company so far out in front that you have moved beyond your competitors. When you go to the beach, you will see many people all over the place (your competition), but when you go into the water, you will see fewer people, and the further out into the ocean you swim, the bluer the water and fewer the competitors. Adding small things to your offerings or unique ways of saying the same thing could be all it takes to move you beyond the competition. I did it by guaranteeing the results of my advertisement. I always told people they could believe what I told them, but I started calling it a "guarantee." I didn't change anything—I simply said it differently and louder. No one had ever guaranteed results in their advertising before. I created a blue ocean, and we grew rapidly.

Shoe Dog by Phil Knight

This is a real-life story about the struggles of moving a business from nothing to success—the hard work, the decisions to be made, and the persistence and time it takes to get where you want to go. This book impressed upon me the benefits of doing business face to face, and since reading it, I have been on the road, meeting my customers in person, and my business is growing by leaps and bounds as a result. It's interesting, too, that our company is the only mail company going out to meet our customers where they are, just like Phil Knight did.

Rocket Fuel by Gino Wickman

This is part one of the *Traction* book I list below. It's an overview of what your business should look like as you begin to understand the importance of hiring the right people and putting them in the right seat based on their natural talents.

Traction by Gino Wickman

Traction is a deep dive into every detail needed to structure your business in an organized, thoughtful approach, starting with you. Once I got out to visit big clients, instead of trying to make every decision in the office, my business started to grow. I don't know what your personality will allow, but this book will help you identify your natural talents and begin the all-important process of hiring the right people and putting them in the right seats to match their natural talents. The strategies in this book provide a system to evaluate the success of each person in your company. Once put in place, you will be amazed at how happy your team will be, and the growth of your company will follow as mine did.

Money: Master the Game by Tony Robbins

Anything written by Tony Robbins is probably worth your time, but this one made my list because it digs deep into the minds of the world's greatest money managers. Tony's celebrity allows him to reach people that others cannot. *Money* will absolutely help you better understand what to do with money once you have it. If you've read the other books on this list and employed the concepts within, you will have money. You should understand how to keep it and how to grow it.

CONCLUSION

I hope some of what you read was interesting and maybe even thought-provoking. I want you to know that I had an ideal childhood, and I aspired to give that to my children. I think I came close to achieving that goal.

My childhood was about growing up with a super-competitive father and a cool older brother who was naturally good at everything he did. My brother Bill was good at every sport he played, and he challenged me to practice more than he did if I wanted to keep up.

Dad was always patient in teaching us all the sports, and he was a master at letting us win just enough that we wanted to keep playing. He knew if we never won, we would likely lose interest. All my dad ever wanted to do was to play with us. Steve, Bill, and I grew up to play soccer, baseball, basketball, tennis, racquetball, ping pong, and pool. Not to mention all the card games Dad would play with us. All while Mom was taking care of all of our other needs. Mom would make you the perfect sandwich without even asking if you wanted one, and she didn't just make a sandwich—it was a piece of art. Lightly toasted bread, plenty of ham or turkey or both with the perfect proportion of Swiss cheese, and always crispy lettuce, thinly sliced tomato, and a smear of mayonnaise—Hellman's for me and Miracle Whip for Steve.

Steve and I were seven years old, and Bill was ten when Mom and Dad told us we were moving for the first time. Our moves always strengthened the family. I think the first move was the easiest for me because of how young I was. It was more traumatic the older I got. Leaving Texas to move to Scottsdale, Arizona, was a lot more difficult because I was twelve years old, in seventh grade, and so unsure of myself. But I never had to go to a new school or the first day of soccer practice all by myself because I always had Steve to go with me since we were twins.

Looking back at the moves we made, they were always for Dad's work as he worked his way up the corporate ladder and excelled in each position he took. Dad was a thinker and a planner—I don't think of him as a risk-taker, but I didn't really know him until I grew up. He was thirty-five years old, and Mom was thirty-four when they moved away from everything they knew to Texas, over 1500 miles away. That was risky. As usual, though, Dad found a way to put his positive spin on everything. He would find a way to make it fun for us while he took on most of the burden.

CONCLUSION

When we were fourteen, Steve and I moved to Dallas for Dad's work, but Bill stayed behind to finish high school, and with that move, everything changed. That move from Scottsdale to Dallas was when I got my own room for the first time. Sure, I missed my big brother, but he was interested in other stuff now anyway, and I finally didn't have to share a room with Steve. Steve and I would eventually share a dorm room at college for two years and create some of the greatest memories I have today. Who knows, maybe we will share a room again in thirty years.

I told you I had an ideal family life, but I also told you that I moved from New York to Texas, Texas to Arizona, Arizona back to Texas, and Texas to Louisiana. Each one of those moves was difficult for me and all of us, but our frame of mind was created by Bill and Lucy. Mom and Dad refused to see things as hard. They were just things we were going to do.

I could have concluded by telling you to use sunscreen every day and not drink soda, which, of course, would be good advice, but now that you have added all of my wonderful knowledge to your big brain, you can decide whether you agree with me or not. And you might not agree with me today, but change your mind when you get older.

The biggest message your Pop has for you is to do everything and try everything. The only things in life you will regret are the things you don't reach for. If you can think of it, then you can do it. So start thinking and start doing. Just remember, your Pop loves you and believes in you. But more importantly, you should believe in yourself.

THANK YOU FOR READING MY BOOK!

LET'S TALK!

Scan the QR code to connect directly with the author!
Ask questions, share your thoughts about the book,
or just say hello—your feedback is always welcome.

Scan the QR Code:

I appreciate your interest in my book and value your feedback as it helps me improve future versions of this book. I would appreciate it if you could leave your invaluable review on Amazon.com with your feedback. Thank you!

www.ingramcontent.com/pod-product-compliance
Lightning Source LLC
Chambersburg PA
CBHW071227160426
43196CB00012B/2435